LINCOLNSHIRE
DIALECT

A selection of words and anecdotes
from around Lincolnshire

by
Lindsey Bourne

BRADWELL
BOOKS

Published by Bradwell Books
9 Orgreave Close Sheffield S13 9NP
Email: books@bradwellbooks.co.uk

British Library Cataloguing in Publication Data:
a catalogue record for this book is available from
the British Library.

1st Edition

ISBN: 9781910551028

Print: Gomer Press, Llandysul, Ceredigion SA44 4JL

Design and artwork by: Andrew Caffrey

Photograph Credits: iStock and North Lincolnshire
Museums Service and credited individually.
www.risbygrangelongwools.co.uk.

Introduction

If you want to really get to know a place, try exploring its dialect. This is certainly true for the county of Lincolnshire. By finding out about the words, phrases and language spoken locally – both past and present – you truly get to understand the character of the county. If you've been 'cantouzled' by Lincolnshire's vivid dialect in the past or 'mazzed' by some of the words you hear in the area, never fear! You can uncover some of the words which make up Lincolnshire language, new and old, right here in our glossary!

Just a brief look at the glossary reveals how much of Lincolnshire's agricultural past lies in its language. If you're keen to try out the dialect for yourself, take a look at our round-up of some great Lincolnshire phrases and sayings. Lincolnshire's dialect is cleverly summed up in the 'Linkisheer Dictionary', a poem written by poet Andy Robinson and proudly featured in this book.

Lincolnshire has a passion for its dialect. This is the county, after all, where the council is so concerned about people not understanding the local dialect that it has set up special workshops. It is also the county where the dialect is celebrated and captured by a dedicated society and by an eccentric farmer! There's no doubting it: this is a county which values the words, phrases and pronunciation that help make it so unique. It is also a place which has inspired many writers, past and present, and which was also the birthplace of one of Queen Victoria's favourite poets.

You know you're in Lincolnshire when being called a 'yellowbelly' is a good thing! Discover why in this book. You can also find out what lies behind some of the county's oldest traditions. There's so much to Lincolnshire and its dialect and history, from its identity as the county captured in one of the most well-known folk songs to being the birthplace of one of the most important figures in the history of computing.

Sadly, there is only so much detail we can go into in this little book, but hopefully it will inspire you to make your own explorations. Whether you're fascinated by words, curious about the history of this diverse county or just keen to learn some interesting old sayings, enjoy the journey!

An old map of Lincolnshire iStock

Glossary

A

A deal – a lot

Aboon – above

Aboot – about

Above – too much for

Addle – to earn

Agateways – to accompany part of the way

Agean/agen/agin – again

Ahint/ahind – behind

Ain – own

Airms – arms

Aisy – easy

Allamort – sunk, dejected, undone

Allus – always

An 'all/ann 'all – and all, also

Anker – to long for

Arpent – witty, smart

Arnt – are not

Arrad – tired

Arsy-varsy – topsy-turvy

Arter – after

Askey – sideways, crooked

Atween – between

Aud/au'd – old

Ax/axe/axed – ask, asked

B

Back end – Autumn

Backerds – backwards

Bad, badly – sick, unwell

Badliness – sickness, illness

Baffle – to put off

Bag – a cow's udder

Bairns – children

Balderdash – nonsense

Batten – bundle of straw

Be'ent/beant – won't, am not, are not, is not

Beer-off – off licence

Behint – behind

Betimes – in time

Bezzle – to drink fast

Bilge – to drink excessively

Blab – to gossip

Blaring – noisy

Blush – to look like another person

Bo'ans/boans – bones

Bobberies/bobbery – disturbance

Bogles/boggles – a ghost

Bog pad – a footpath

Boke – to be sick

Bonny – healthy

Bont – burnt

Brain-pan – skull

Brame – bramble, brier

Brashy – brittle

Brat – child

Braunge – haughty

Broodle – to cherish

Brussen – fill up

Bundelt/bundled – to remove quickly

Bust – broken

By and by – after a time, shortly

C

Cadge – to carry

Cantouzle – to derange, confound

Catblash – thin and poor

Cep – except

Chats – small things, or small bits of anything

Chatterbags/Chitterbags – a chatterbox

Childer – children

Chip – to squabble, quarrel

Cho'ch – church

Chump/Chumpy – broad, stout

Claggy – sticky, clogging

Clam – to starve

Clarted – dirty, muddy or messy

Clatty – fiddling with something

Clean – quite, completely

Clem – hungry

Clifty – generous

Clitch – a brood of young chickens

Closin's/cloasin's/cloasen – an enclosure

Clotty – to speak or act foolishly

Clotty-box – chatter-box

Clouts – working clothes, rag or cloth

Cobby – brisk, lively

Coldrick – used to describe a person who can't bear being cold

Collyfogle – wheedle, cheat

Coney/cony – rabbit

Coom/coomed/come – arrive, arrived

Coos – cows

Coshy – squashy

Cot – caught

Cottered/cotted – matted, knotted (particularly referring to hair)

Crake – a crow

Crappely – lame

Creed meal/creed wheat – wheat simmered until soft and tender for making frumenty, a medieval dish made from cracked wheat

Crooded/croodle – to nestle or snuggle

Croom'led – crumbled, crumpled

Crouncy – frisky in a horse

Cusinet – pincushion

Crysoms/chrisom/chrislom – delicate, weak

D

Daff, Daffy – doughy

Dagbite – meat between meals

Dallack – to dress smartly and gaudily

Darklins – just twilight

Darter – daughter

Dawl – to tire

Deary/dearie – small

Deedy – industrious or notable

Delve – to work hard

Dessably – constantly

Ditted – dirty, grimy

Dog-poor – very poor, extremely poor

Dog shelf – the floor

Doon – down

Doorsil/door sill – threshold

Doorstud/doorstead – door step

Drawed – drawn, drew

Dree – drawn out, tedious

Druv – driven, drove

Dwined/dwyne – dwindled

Dyke – ditch or drain

Lincoln Cathedral
towers above the
shops and houses
iStock

E

Ear – the handle of a cup, or jug

Earning – rennet

Easement – relief

Eddish – the aftercrop of grass after the hay-crop has been cut

Efter – after

Eke – to lengthen

Elder – a cow's udder

Endlong – go directly forward, continuously

Enew – enough

Esh – ash-tree

Eyne/eyen/ein/eyn/een – eyes

F

Faather – father

Fair – absolutely, level, even

Fairy ring – a circle in grass believed to be made by fairies dancing

False roof – attic or loft

Far-length – distance, furthest length

Farweltered – in some kind of difficulty, apparently derived from a term for a sheep which has rolled over onto its back and got stuck

Fasten-Tuesday, or Fasten Eve – Shrove Tuesday, the Eve

of the Fast of Lent

Fatted/fat – to fatten

Fause – false, cunning

Feat, featish – neat, nice, well-done

Fellowship – friendly conversation

Fetch – a trick, a device,

Fett – to secure or tie firmly

Feyther – father

Fiddle – jam pastry

Fierce – brisk, lively

First off – for the first thing, the beginning

Fitter – a small piece or fragment

Fittie – a small holiday bungalow

Flacket – a small wooden barrel, used for beer by labourers in harvest

Flinged – throw, overturn

Flit – to flee or steal away in the night.

Floutin/flouter/flowter – to say bad things to or about anyone, to scold

Fluster/flusker – excited, hurried

Fo'ak/fooak – folk

Force-put – a matter of necessity

Fore-elders – forefathers, ancestors

Forenoon – the later hours before noon, as distinct from the morning or earliest part of the day

Forset – to upset

Forspell – put a spell on/bewitch

Frae/fra – from

Fratchy – fretful, peevish, restless

Fridge – to fray, chafe

Froighted – frightened

Fund/fun – found

Fur – for or far

Furder – further

G

Gain/gainhand – near

Gain – pretty, very, nearly

Gainly – handy, clever

Garth – yard, stackyard

Geyan/gean – near

Gillery – deceit, trickery, cheating

Gi'n/gi'en/gin/gen – given

Girn/gern – grin

Git – to get

Glower/gloar/glore – to stare vacantly

Gob/gob-hole – mouth

Gotten – possess, obtain, got

Grade'ly – excellent, thorough, handsome, true

Gran'ther – grandfather

Grat/greet/grete – to shed tears, to weep

Grow'd/growed/growd – grew

Gy'arden – garden

H

Happed/hapt oop/hap-up – wrapped up, covered up

Happing – covering

Hark – harken

Hawiver – however

Heerd – heard

Hevent/hevna – haven't

Hirings – statute fairs for hiring servants

Hissen – himself

Hoam – home

Hoo – how

Hoose/hoos – house

Hunnerds, hunderds – hundreds

Hurted/hurten – hurt

I

Ill – bad

Ill-convenient – inconvenient

Ill-gain – inconvenient, unhandy

In co – used commonly for in partnership

In detriment – detriment, harm, damage

Ing – a low-lying meadow

Insense – to inform, give or gain information

Isel/izel – smuts from the fire

Ivery, Iv'ry – ivy

Ivery/ivvry – every

J

Jack up – to throw over

Jacket – to beat, thrash

Jacketing – a beating, thrashing

Jay-bird – a Jay

The Seal of the
City of Boston
in 1575
Shutterstock ©meunierd

Jenny-run-by-the-ground – ground ivy

Jet – to strut, jerk about

Jiffle – to wriggle or move about

Jigger – to tire out

Jiggle – to jog, or shake about

Jitty/Jetty – a narrow passage between houses

Joist/jeist – to pasture out stock on another's land for hire

Jolly – fat, large

Jug – a stone bottle, such as is used for wine or spirits, not a milk-jug

Jut – to jolt

K

Keb – to sob

Kedge-bellied – pot-bellied

Keel – the name given to barges on the Trent

Keep/keeping – food for sheep and cattle

Kegged – grown and matted together

Kegmeg – refuse, offal commonly used of bad food

Kelch – a thump, blow said of a violent fall

Kelter – rubbish, litter, junk, debris

Ken/kenned – to know

Kep – kept or keep

Kevass/keviss – to run up and down, romp about

Kibble – the knobbed stick or bat used in the game of

Knur, Spell, and Kibble

Kid – a bundle of sticks tied up for firewood

Kill – a kiln

Kilp, or pot-kilp – the iron handle by which a pot or bucket is hung

Kimy – fusty, tainted

Kin-cough, kink-cough – the whooping-cough

Kirkgarth – churchyard

Sailing boats moored in a tidal river at low tide
iStock

Kit – a large wooden vessel for holding milk

Kitling – a kitten

Knag, gnag, nag – to gnaw, tease, worry, scold

Knagger – a teaser

Knap – to snap, break short off

Knap-knee'd – knock-kneed

Knawed – knew

Knit – to unite, join together

Knoll – to toll, as a church bell for a funeral

Knop – the round head or bud of a plant

Knopped – partly dried, rough dried; usually referred to washed clothes

Knowed/knewed – did know

Knur – the wooden ball, or knot of wood, struck with the kibble in the game of knur, spell and kibble

L

Lace – to mix spirits with tea

Lafft – laugh

Land – the ridge or raised ground between the furrows in a field, thrown up by ploughing

Landed – covered with soil

Land-horse – the near horse which, in ploughing with a pair of horses, walks on the smoother unploughed land, as distinguished from the off, or furrow, horse

Lane-ends – crossroads

Lankrel/langrel – lanky, tall and thin

Lanthorn – lantern

Lap – to wrap, cover

Latter-end – the latter part of the year

Launch out – to fling or throw out

Lawks/laws – explanation of surprise

Lay – a parish rate or levy

Laylock – lilac

Lead – to carry with horse and cart

Leastwise/leastways – at least

Lee – lye, or water mixed with wood ashes for washing

Length – to do as one likes

Lether – Ladder

Lief, Liever – soon, willingly, rather

Lig – to lie

Like – have to, be content to

Limber – pliant, flexible

Limmock – pliant, flexible

Limpelty-lobelty – limber, flexible

Ling – the common name for heather

Lints – lentils

Lire – to plait

Lithe – to thicken milk or broth with flour or oatmeal

Liver – to deliver

Lob – to eat noisily

Lode – a drain or watercourse

Lop – a flea

Lope – to leap

Lose the end of – to be without knowledge or tidings of

Lost – utterly neglected, at a loss

Low – short

Lowance – allowance: beer allowed in return for work

Luck-penny – a small sum of money returned for luck on a purchase

Lug hole – ear

Lunge – to lounge, idle about

Lungeous – ill-tempered, spiteful

Lusky – lazy, idle

M

Main – a lot

Mappen/may'appen/may happen – perhaps

Mardy – sullen or bad tempered

Marrer – close friend, used in place of 'mate', or 'the other one of a pair'

Mash – to brew a pot of tea

Maze – frighten, astonish

Mazzed/mazzled/mazeded/mazzarded – bewildered, stupefied, confused

Mazy – dizzy, giddy

Mazzen/mazzle – stupify, make dizzy

Mebbe – maybe, perhaps

Meddle – interfere

Mek – make

Mend the grate – mind or tend to the fire

Mind – to call to memory

Misloike/mislike – dislike

Mither – to complain or grumble

Mold – earth, soil

Moocky – misty, dull, muggy

Mort – lot of

Mowt – might

Moysed – amazed, bewildered

Mun – must

N

Nagnail – a corn

Nasty – ill-tempered, cross

Nation – very, exceedingly

Nat'rally – naturally

Natter/knatter – peevish, fretful

Natty – tidy, neat, trim

Nature – natural substance or virtue

Naw/nay/naay – no

Nayther/naaither/nauther – neither

Near – mean, close, stingy.

Neb – a bird's bill or a nose

Neglectful – negligent

Neighbouring – visiting and gossiping with one's neighbours

Nesh – susceptible to the cold; soft, tender, delicate

Nestle – to fidget

Newsing – gossiping

Newsy – fond of news, gossiping

Nice/niced/neist – particular, fastidious.

Nicker – a woodpecker

Nickers – the larger branches of tree tops, cut up for firewood

Nigh – near

Nip – to move about quickly, to be nimble

Nithered – to be extremely cold

Niver/nivver – never

Nobbut/nobut – nothing but, only

No-but – nothing but

Noggin – a thick slice or wedge, as of bread, pudding etc.

None so – not so

Noo – now

Nor – than

Nothing – not at all

Nowt – nothing

O

O'an sel – myself
On – of
Oot – out
Owd/ohd – old
Ower/oher – over
Owt/ought – anything

P

Pad – path
Peewit – lapwing
Pine – starve
Pore – of bad quality or thin
Pother – bother, a bustle
Puggle – to stir (a stick used for stirring is known as a 'puggling' stick)

Q

Quavery – undecided
Quicks – thorns, young plants

R

Ramper/ramp – to rush about violently

Reetly/reightly – certainly, exactly

Reglar/regular – a versatile word to emphasise the following word, similar to 'great' or 'good'

Roon/roond – near

Rue – repent

S

Saft/safe – sure

Sartain/sartan/sartin – certain

Sartan-sewer – quite certain

Scrammell'd/ scrawmled – crawled

Seed – saw

Settle – a seat

Showther/shou'ther – shoulder

Shy – deceitful

Sich – such

Siling – to rain extremely hard

Sin – since

Skirl – to shriek

Snaggy – rough

Snape/sneep – not right

Sneepit/snerp – to shrivel

Sore – bad

Spinney – a narrow strip of land

Spud – a small implement used to cut thistles

Starved – to be extremely cold

Stead/steed – instead

Stoan – stone

Stot – stumble

Straange – strange

Strong – great, large

Stummelt – stumbled

Stummick – stomach

Summat/summut – something

Sweer – to swear

T

Tack – taste or taint

Ta'en – taken

Ta'en-work – work taken by the piece or job

Tailings, tail-ends – the leftover parts of corn deemed not fit for market, but kept to feed farm animals

Taking – difficulty, dilemma, condition

Tang – a sting

Tar-marl, tar-marline – tarred cord used by gardeners

'Tates, taets – potatoes

Team – to lead, or carry with wagon and horses

Teaty – fretful

Teem – to empty

Telit/tell'd/tellt – told

Temse – sieve

Tent – to tend, or look after

Tew – to harass or weary

Thack – thatch, to thatch

Thacker – thatcher

Thick – friendly, intimate

Thick-end – the greater part

Think much – to envy, begrudge

Tho'en, th a wen – thawed

Thoff – though

Thou – you

Thowt – thought

Throff/thruf – through

Throng – busy

Thrum – to purr

Thusky, thusking – big, large, used to describe a person

Tickle – uncertain, not dependable

Tiddy – small

Toft, toft-stead – a piece of ground on which a house stands or has stood

To'n/ton – turn

To'nup – turnip

Topping – in good health, excellent

Torndown – a loud rough person

Towanst/wonst – once

Town-end – the end of a village

Town-street – the road which runs through a village

To-year, to-month – this year, this month

Trace – to wander, or walk aimlessly about

Trail – to drag, draw

Traily – weary

Translator – a term for a cobbler, who works up old shoes into new ones

Trape, or trapes – to run idly and skittishly about

Traun – truant

Trouble – pain

Turn – to begin to recover from sickness

Turnover – a type of small shawl

Tush, or tushipeg – tooth

Twining – twisting

Twitterin'- nervous, frightened

U

Ugly, ugliness – disagreeable, disagreeableness

Unbeknown – not known

Under – not up to

Underbrush – underwood

Underlout – the weaker or inferior

Unhapped, unheppen – awkward, clumsy

Useter, used ter – did once

W

Waffy, wafflin'- silly, weak, ineffectual

Wanst, wonst – once

Wark – work

Wetchered – to be wet through

Wheer's – where's

While – until

Whisht – be quiet

Wi' 'em – with them

Will o' tha wykes/will o' th' wisp/willerby-wisp – the name for ignis fatuus, the self-igniting marsh gas found in wetland which appeared as small flickering flames on the water

Winder, winda – window

Wi'out – without

Wor – were

Worrit – to worry

Wuss/wo's – worse

Y

Yaller, yalla, yallow – yellow

Yarbs, yerbs – herbs

Yarth, yearth – earth

Yit – yet

Yond/yon – yonder

Lincolnshire sayings and phrases

Every county has its own set of sayings, and Lincoln-shire is no different. As the strange power of language dictates, you may have heard some of these in other parts of the country. While many sayings hail from Lincolnshire's past, others are clearly more modern.

All my eye and Peggy Martin – Wasted talk. This saying is thought to come from the time when British sailors were attacking Spanish ships.

It's black over Bill's mothers – It looks like it's going to rain.

Fasten, or fastening penny – The money given to 'fasten' or confirm a bargain or hiring at the hiring and mop fairs. You can read more about this tradition later on in this book!

I ged a shilling fasten-penny.
He sent back his fasten-penny.
He tell'd him he might drink his fasten-penny.
He ged the mester back his fasten-penny.

From *A Glossary of Words used in South-West Lincolnshire, Wapentake of Graffoe* by ROBERT EDEN GEORGE COLE, published in 1886.

Course of the country – To see the world.

Daft as a boiled owl – No use to anyone.

Do you come from Bardney? – You left the door open!

Duck – Used in Lincolnshire and other areas of the county to show mild affection.

Going down under/down below – Fishermen once used this term around the Boston area to mean 'fishing in the Wash' shallows, just below the low water line.

Everything but the squeak – Not for the squeamish, this is thought to be derived from the act of killing a pig and using all of it, except the squeak!

Evvy egg a bod – Every egg a bird, i.e. there's one for everyone.

Firkle about – To search for something.

Flitting Day – The day when a person leaves their old employer for a new one. Often associated with the hiring fairs of the past.

Fogo as a fummard – Something smells very strongly!

Friday-best o' days, worst o' days – Used when referring to Fridays.

From clogs to clogs in three generations – Refers to the pattern of a man working or finding his way to wealth, passing it on to his son, only to have it wasted by the third generation.

Go to the foot of our stairs – Used as an expression of exasperation.

God'e'en – Good evening

Gone out – Surprised.

Hang your nose over – To look something over for a long time.

It's a bag o' moonshine – It's a load of nonsense!

He's got all his buttons on, but they're all on one side – He's all about his own interests.

He got up backside first – He's in a bad mood.

He's cut his mouth on a brocken bottle – He talks posh!

He talks as he warms – He gets more enthusiastic.

He was come day, go day, God send Sunday – He is unreliable

He wants to know far end o' Meg/Meg's backside – He's very inquisitive.

His collar was so high he had to stand up to spit – Used to describe someone wearing a very stiff or high collar.

If he fell off Burton's, he'd land in a suit! – He's very lucky!

I wish I had hold of our cat's tail – I wish I was at home!

I'll do it before I screw my leg off – It needs to be done immediately.

It's Jack Hawkins' day – it keeps coming and going – Rain is on its way!

Least of time – In a moment, in the very shortest time.

New Year's Day – The saying about this day said 'Bring a bit of green into the house on New Year's Day, and you won't want bread all the year.' If you did, somebody would bring you some! Another belief was that whatever you bring in first on New Year's Day, you will never lack all the year through. This was why the tradition was to bring in coals or food or something else which was considered useful.

Nip up or nip off – To snatch up quickly.

Pearls bring tears – Used when referring to pearls.

Ride bareback to Paris on it – Used to describe a blunt knife.

She has a stiff row to hoe – She has a difficult time ahead of her.

To side the table – to clear the dishes from the table.

Take the wrong way – used to refer to an ill person who is getting worse instead of better.

Ten foot – The alley way between houses or behind houses.

A time or two – once or twice.

Think they will – a common term for like, choose.

Town-row – By town-tow, or by house-row, was the term for the old way of keeping men off the parish when there wasn't much work. This was done by finding them so many days' work at each farm in turn.

Where did Lincoln get its name?

It is believed that Lincoln takes its name from the Celtic word 'Lindon', which means 'pool by the hill'. This is thought to refer to the Brayford Pool and the hill on which Lincoln stands today. It was in the Viking period that Lincoln really came into its own in terms of trade and you can still see evidence of its Viking past in street names such as Flaxengate and Danesgate. Speaking of place names, if you hear people talking about 'Ming-Ming' these days, they will be locals of Immingham, using their local nickname for the place! On the other hand, if you overhear people talking about 'Meg', it could be residents of Metheringham referring to where they live!

Yellowbellies and proud!

It's a fact: Lincolnshire is the home of the yellowbelly or *'yellerbelly'*. This is the name that Lincolnshire people are proud to give themselves. But where does this unusual nickname come from? Well, there are a number of theories, some of which sound more plausible than others ... perhaps the mystery behind the name will never be conclusively resolved, but one thing is for sure: it will continue to excite debate amongst Lincolnshire people for many years to come.

Blame it on the frogs, newts and eels?

In the depths of the Lincolnshire Fens it is said that there lives a breed of newt, frog or eel which has a yellow underside or belly.

Grose's *A Provincial Glossary; with a Collection of Local Proverbs etc*, 1787, says:

> *'Yellow bellies. This is an appellation given to persons born in the Fens, who, it is jocularly said, have yellow bellies, like their eels.'*

Could this be the secret behind the mysterious name?

A Sheepish Tale?

Cathedral Shearlings Louise Fairburn www.risbygrangelongwools.co.uk

Some people think that the name may be based on another creature, namely the Lincoln Longwool Sheep. As you might have guessed from the name, the Lincoln Longwool, traditional to the county, is blessed with a particularly long coat. These lovely sheep were known to have grazing grounds in fields of mustard. You can guess the result of all that wool dragging around in the mustard flowers...

Hard-working farmers?

During the long hot summer months Lincolnshire's farmers would often work without their shirts on in order to keep cool. As they tended the fields they would be bent over, naturally gaining a suntan on their backs. In contrast, their fronts would be less exposed and would stay white. This theory seems a little topsy-turvy when you think about it! Another version suggests that it is the reflection of the corn which was thought to have given a yellow glow to the farmers' stomachs, hence the name!

You've got mail?

Is the post to blame for the unusual Lincolnshire nickname? It is said that the Lincoln to London mail coach had a bright yellow undercarriage. When it arrived in London, people would shout out *'Here comes the Lincolnshire yellowbelly!'*

In other versions of this theory, it is said that the coach was the Lincoln to York rather than the Lincoln to London.

THE LOUTH MAIL SNOWED UP. 1836—THE LETTER-BAGS ARE SENT ON IN A POST CHAISE AND FOUR
J. Pollard

The Louth mail coach snowed up in 1836, as illustrated in
The Graphic in 1888 iStock

The military connection?

Is the nickname actually all about the clothing worn by Lincolnshire's military men? A number of theories have grown around this angle. One is that 'yellowbelly' comes from the yellow sashes worn by Lincolnshire Regiment soldiers. Another is that it is inspired by the colour of the waistcoats worn by the Royal North Lincolnshire Militia officers. Yet another theory, uncovered as recently as 2009, is that it was inspired by the clothing worn by the soldiers of the 30th Regiment of the Line, who were recruited from Lincolnshire amongst other places. Their uniform had yellow facings.

However, there is still another take on the military theory. This one goes that during the American war of Independence, the Lincolnshires were trapped in an area of swampland. They scrabbled through the undergrowth to keep out of sight and escape safely. When they eventually did escape, they were caked in the local mud, which happened to be yellow... The theory goes that they were called Lincolnshire Yellowbellies from then on!

All in the place name?

One theory suggests that the nickname came from the name for the Rural Deanery which served the Fen part of the Lincoln Diocese; this came from the Saxon Wapentake, referred to as *'Ye Elloe Bellie'*. It seems that Elloe means 'out of the morass' and bel was the Celtic word for hole or hollow. The original yellowbellies were perhaps then the inhabitants of the Fens. and the name gradually became adopted for people from all areas of Lincolnshire.

From the poppy?

Did the name come from a more sinister source? One theory goes that Malaria was common in the Fens and local people took opium as a medicine, which gave their skin a yellow hue.

Pirate vests?

Could the name have come from locals in Cleethorpes who, many years ago, lit lights to lure passing ships to the rocks and take their cargo? The story goes that one night when they were doing this, they discovered that the cargo was an abundance of yellow flannel fabric! Because they had to be discreet about their finds, the local people turned the fabric into vest-type garments which turned them into yellowbellies …

The gold sovereign?

Was the nickname inspired by a local custom? It is thought that it was once the tradition amongst Lincolnshire families to hang a gold sovereign around the neck of their first-born male child.

Mustard-coloured?

Yet another theory is that the nickname developed when workers in the mustard fields became covered in pollen from the mustard flowers.

A splendid field of mustard in full bloom iStock

Spud Stains?

Another theory that brings in Lincolnshire's agricultural history is the one in which the farm workers were picking potatoes and used their shirt bottoms or aprons to gather them in, gaining a kind of yellow belly in the process!

Local Traditions

Lincolnshire Day

Lincolnshire Day is a relatively new tradition which aims to celebrate all things Lincolnshire. The day, first celebrated in 2006, marks the anniversary of the Lincolnshire Rising in 1536, in which the Catholics revolted against the establishment of the Church of England by HENRY VIII. Thankfully, the event itself, now celebrated annually on 1 October, is very much a peaceful, positive affair, celebrating Lincolnshire's traditions with special events of all kinds.

Scunthorpe United F.C. during season 1904–1905, taken by Arthur Singleton ©North Lincolnshire Museums Service

What were the Mop and Hiring Fairs?

Now, the **Mop Fair** may sound like some kind of strange festival which celebrates a domestic implement. But it was actually a big part of life in many parts of the country. It all started with the hiring fairs, or, as they were also known, the statute fairs. These took place every year in most rural towns. They were the time of the year in which the people seeking domestic servants would come together with potential candidates. The hiring fairs took place on 11 November, which was Martinmas Day.

It seems that in Lincolnshire the agreement between the new servant and their master was sealed by the handing over of what was called the fasten-penny (this was customarily a shilling), which 'fastened' the contract for twelve months. A few days after this event, the Mop Fair would be held. It was also known as the Runaway Mop. The name Mop is thought to be derived from the Old English word for a tassel or tuft. The name perhaps comes from the badges or tufts which were worn by the people looking for work, each rag symbolising the type of job they had.

A less kind theory about the name suggests that it comes from the old meaning of the word mop as referring to a fool, a comment on this fair being for people who weren't sharp enough to find an employer at the main hiring fair!

The mop fair continues to this day in some parts of the country, but it is now about having fun rather than finding a job!

The only eight-sailed traditional windmill remaining in Heckington, Lincolnshire. It was built in around 1830. iStock

Another part of this local tradition which has almost been forgotten is **Pag Rag Day** on 14 May. This was the day on which servants left home carrying all their laundry in a bag – their pag bag. Pag Rag Day was focused around taking on new servants and farm workers.

Cleaning time

Cleaning time was the period just before old May Day. During this time, home-owners gave their homes a regular annual cleaning, before their farm servants, who were employed from May Day to May Day, left their positions.

Front door

It is said that in the Lincolnshire of the past, the first door of every home must only be used for three things: a new baby, a bride or a coffin.

Gooding

Also known as *'thomasing'* or *'mumping'*, this was the tradition in which women would go out begging for corn or money on St. Thomas's' Day for the Christmas Feast.

The Horncastle Horse Fair

A well-established custom in Horncastle was its horse fair, held every August and known around the world. It was so popular that it continued right up until the end of World War II.

The Stamford Bull Run

'Come all you bonny boys,
Who love to bait the bonny bull,
Who take delight in noise,
And you shall have your belly-full,
On Stamford's Town Bull Running Day,
We'll show you such right gallant play,
You never saw the like, you'll say,
As you have seen at Stamford.'

'The Stamford Bullards', FOLK SONG

Animals played another part in the traditions of Lincolnshire in the Stamford Bull Run festival which took place in Stamford every 13 November. Legend has it that the tradition goes back to an incident when William de Warenne, 5th Earl of Surrey, noticed two bulls fighting in a meadow. A number of butchers were called in to deal with the fight and one of the bulls headed straight for the town. The earl found this all rather entertaining and gave the meadow to the butchers of Stamford on the condition that they should provide a bull, to be run in the town every 13 November, in perpetuity. The town of Stamford acquired common rights in the grassy flood plain next to the Welland. This was known as Bull Meadow right up to the last century. Anyone who cares about animal welfare will be glad to hear that this tradition ended in 1839. A more humane version of the custom took place in 2013 when the Bull Run was re-enacted with puppets.

A blacksmith's shop in Barrow-on-Humber in the 1920s
©North Lincolnshire Museums Service

Capturing the voices of Lincolnshire's past

A new project is helping to bring Lincolnshire's dialect and traditions to life. The Village Voices project is uncovering even more of the county's past by making an audio record of Lincolnshire's history. The lottery-funded project is working to share the real-life stories of rural life in northern and eastern Lincolnshire. Local people can get involved by taking part in special 'reminiscence sessions' in libraries and village halls. The project is run by North East Lincolnshire Library Service and is helping to create an archive of stories from local people. The project has already led to the creation of four radio-style documentaries.

Linkisheer Dictionary

We all love wods and dialects
That's why we're here todaäy
Each one's a little different
So here's my Linkisheer way

I'll try and educaäte yar
Or as we would call it larn
Maybe some of it'll rub off
When yar've eeärd this little yarn

Now if a bairn is crying
We would say it's beeäling.
A check now he lives in a sty
All full of grunts and squeäling.

Skwad is the word for muddy
When the land is wet and squelchin'
Resulting from some heavy rain
Known locally as kelchin'

The verb to lie we would say
Should really be to lig
And the humble earwig seen by all
Is called a battletwig.

A gansey is a coät

Or woolly to keep yar waarm
In winter I might put one on
For working on the farm.

To gawster is to belly-laugh
At someone's joke or jape
And kelter is just rubbish
Like European red tape.

A Skegness pigeon behind the plough
Is nowt but a hungry seagull
And 'Ah'm brussen as an 'arvest toäd'
Tells yar that me belly's full.

A maggot it becomes a mawk
In our way of talkin'
And a simple scarecrow
To us is just a mawkin.

People who move in from far away
Are outners or frim-foäk
And if it's black ower Feyther's taätes
Then we're in for a soäk

When yar go to feed the cattle
Yar off ter gath the beäst
And going to a dog-hanging

46

That's a party or a feäst.

Sometimes a 'th' becomes a 'd'
And a path becomes a pad
And an owd boy ain't allust owd
Sometimes he's just a lad.

Yar'll get wetchered when wi'out a coät
Y'are caught in rainy weather
A 'd', well that becomes 'th'
And ladder becomes lether

To yar it may seem straänge
Some of the wods we saäy
At night-time after hours of work
We'll loase off fer the day.

In summertime the sun shines
Boäth sides the hedges all day long
A busy day at work is explained
By saying yar've been throng.

Someone who is rayther ill
Is looking straängeing meän
But when it's said he's meggering
Perhaps the doctor he has seän.

Round my way it's a causey
To some that may be a patio
To get a kelch around the lug
Now that's a painful blow.

The frosty morns in winter
Make the pavements rather slaäpe
And summat said to be squayatched
Has been bent out of shaäpe.

What I would call a tup
Yar may call a ram
And a sheep known as a gimmer
Has never had a lamb.

A rack for feeding cattle
Would have the name of heck;
A field-corner or a door-latch
Around me is called a sneck.

To orm about is acting daft
To mantle is to wander.
We don't say 'It's over there',
We say, 'It's ower yonder.'

If owt's complicated or a fuss
A stitherum that would be

Why would yar say owt else?
It's obvious to me.

An otchin it's an 'edge'og
It couldn't be much plaäiner
When coming home or getting nearer
We say we're getting gaäiner.

Mucky owry owd weather
Means a daäy of wind an rain and fog.
If someone's getting on a bit
They're as owd as God's dog.

When East wind blows from North Sea
We'd say, 'It's a bit 'unch.'
When someone's grumpy and not
soäciable
We'd simply call him clunch.

If ever I say 'Sool 'im!'
I'll be setting on a dog.
Yar don't poke summat wi' a stick
Yar give the thing a brog.

So use wods larned at Feyther's knee
Whether yar be lass or lad
Or one day they may disappear

And then yar'll wish you had.

Yar've all got words of yer own
Of that there's nothing surer
If lost within the mists of time
Mother tongue will be the poorer.

Born and raäised, farmed all me life,
Perched high upon the Wold,
Larning the wods and phraäses
And stories I've been told.

This is but a little skerrig
Of the things within me 'eeäd
And I hope as I can use 'em
Ivvery day until I'm deeäd.

The day will come, not yet I hope,
When I have spent my worth
And then forever shall I rest
Wrapped snug in Lincoln earth.

BILLY WOLDSWORTH
Written for the **National Dialect Day**, 2014
Rydal Hall, Cumbria

Mud and stud

Mud and stud may sound like some kind of unusual musical genre, but it's actually the name of architectural style considered by many to be unique to Lincolnshire. You can spot a mud and stud cottage by its central chimney stack, central door and half-hipped thatched roof. While the timbers used to be mainly made of oak prior to the 18th century, the framework tended to be made of pine from then on. Sadly, many mud and stud buildings have been destroyed or neglected over the years. Now, just around 500 survive, with approximately half of those being Grade II and II* listed. Quite a number of Lincolnshire's surviving mud and stud cottages are enjoying a second life as popular holiday homes. Interestingly, you can also find mud and stud buildings in some of the earliest settlements in the USA. This is because carpenters from Lincolnshire travelled to the area, taking their skills with them.

Writing Lincolnshire

Lincolnshire's language and customs have been captured in writing for many years. In fact, as far back as the twelfth century, a poet called Geoffrey Gaimar wrote The Lay of Havelok in the Lincolnshire dialect. Structured in rhyming couplets, this poem has an incredible story behind it. It was believed to be lost for centuries, then a copy of it was suddenly discovered in the Bodleian Library at Oxford in the 19th century! The roots of the poem are believed to lie in a story by Gildas, a 6th-century monk. The poem recounts the tale of the legend of Grim (who established Grimsby) and Havelok, the Danish prince who went on to become King of England and Denmark.

Lincolnshire has been captured in words in the well-known poem *'The High Tide on the Coast of Lincolnshire'* by JEAN INGELOW who was born in Boston. Nor should we forget *'The Lincolnshire Poacher'*, which we will look at it in more detail shortly!

Lincolnshire's own war poet

When you consider the history of Lincolnshire's language, one name stands out in particular: that of BERNARD GILBERT. Born in Billinghay in 1882, Gilbert started out working in his father's seed merchant business, but it wasn't long before his natural talent for writing showed itself. Much of his

iStock

work was written in Lincolnshire dialect and his focus was on local places and themes. Gilbert was soon seeing his work published. Later on, he sold the seed company to focus full-time on his writing. It was then that he really came into his own as a writer. It was with World War I poems such as *'Belgium 1914'* and *'I Have No Ring'* that Bernard Gilbert's reputation as Lincolnshire's own war poet was sealed. He is commemorated with a plaque in St Michael's Church in Billinghay. Writing and literature is something of a Gilbert family tradition, with Bernard's son MICHAEL GILBERT becoming an acclaimed crime writer and his granddaughter HARRIETT GILBERT presenting A Good Read on BBC Radio 4.

Excerpt from *'When I Wor Young'* by Bernard Gilbert

Eene Mene Mina Mo,
Erika Terika Tiny Toe,
Umpsy Bumpsy Staggery One,
One, Two, Three, and out goes she.

In winter time upon our pond,
Of slidin' I wor allers fond;
An' when at last I larnt to skaate,
I used to set the fastest raate.

Besides, we 'ad sich 'eaps o' fun,
To snowball fights we'd truant run;
While Christmas, wi' its merry chimes,
Meant gaames, an' toys, an' jolly times.

Ooats an' beeans an' barley mow,
Ooats an' beeans an' barley mow,
Do you or I or anyone know
'Ow ooats an' beeans an' barley grow ?

But after winter comes the spring,
When flowers bud and birds do sing,
When suddenly wi' noisy shout,
The tops an' hoops come rollin' out.
An' when 'owd March's breezes wild
Begin to raage, then ivery child
Is busy workin' dark an' light,
To see who 'ez the biggest kite.

Bernard Gilbert

Mr. Bernard Gilbert is one of the discoveries of the War. For years,
it seems, he has been writing poetry, but it is only recently that an
inapprehensive country has awakened to the fact. Now he is taking
his rightful place among our foremost singers. What William

Barnes was to Dorset, what T. E. Brown was to the Manx people – this is Mr Gilbert to the folk of his native county of Lincoln. He has interpreted their lives, their sorrows, their aspirations, with a surprising fidelity. Mr Gilbert never loses his grip upon realities. One feels that he knows the men of whom he writes in their most intimate moods; knows, too, their defects, which he does not shrink from recording. There is little of the dreamy idealism of the South in the peasant people of Lincolnshire. The outwardly respectable chapel-goer who asks himself, in a moment of introspection:

But why not have a good time here?
Why should the Devil have all the beer?

is true to type. But he has, too, his softer moods. Fidelity in friendship, courage, resource and perseverance – these are typical of the men of the Fens.

From *The New Witness* magazine, excerpt from *Introduction to Rebel Verses* by BERNARD GILBERT

Lincolnshire continues to be an inspiration for writers today, with a plethora of writers based in the county.

The Lincolnshire Poacher

'*The Lincolnshire Poacher*' is known as the unofficial anthem of Lincolnshire. As with many folk songs, it has evolved over the years, with different versions appearing at various times. However it is believed to go as far back as 1775. Another interesting fact about *'The Lincolnshire Poacher'* is that it was a favourite of King George IV.

These days, the song gives its name to a number of pubs and to a local cheese made at Ulceby Grange in Alford.

You can hear a version of *'The Lincolnshire Poacher'* on the British Council website: http://film.britishcouncil.org/the-lincolnshire-poacher

When I was bound apprentice in famous Lincolnshire
'Twas well I served my master for nigh on seven years
Till I took up to poaching as you shall quickly hear
Oh, 'tis my delight on a shiny night in the season of the year.

As me and my companions was setting out a snare
'Twas then we spied the gamekeeper, for him we didn't care
For we can wrestle and fight, my boys, and jump from anywhere
Oh, 'tis my delight on a shiny night in the season of the year.

As me and my companions was setting four or five
And taking them all up again, we caught a hare alive
We caught a hare alive, my boys, and through the woods did steer
Oh, 'tis my delight on a shiny night in the season of the year.

We threw him over my shoulder, boys, and then we trudged home
We took him to a neighbour's house and sold him for a crown
We sold him for a crown, my boys, but I divven't tell you where
Oh, 'tis my delight on a shiny night in the season of the year.

Success to every gentleman that lives in Lincolnshire
(Alt. Bad luck to every magistrate that lives in Lincolnshire)
Success to every poacher that wants to sell a hare
Bad luck to every gamekeeper that will not sell his deer
Oh, 'tis my delight on a shiny night in the season of the year.

An engraving of the Newport Arch or Gate, the remains of a 3rd-century Roman gate in the city of Lincoln. It is believed to be the oldest arch in the United Kingdom still used by traffic! iStock

Odd & unusual place names in Lincolnshire

Antons Gowt
Ashby de la Launde
Ashby Puerorum
Aslackby
Bag Enderby
Barlings
Beesby in the Marsh
Belchford
Belleau
Benniworth
Bicker
Bigby
Binbrook
Bishop Norton
Bitchfield
Blackjack
Boothby Graffoe
Boothby Pagnell
Brandy Wharf
Brant Broughton
Brauncewell
Burton Coggles
Burton Penwardine
Buslingthorpe
Butterwick
Byards Leap
Candlesby
Carlton Scroop

Cawkwell
Cherry Willingham
Claxby Pluckacre
Clixby
Cold Hamworth
Cowbit
Donna Nook
Dry Doddington
Eagle
Fillingham
Fishtoft
Friskney
Gayton le Marsh
Gedney Drove End
Gipsey Bridge
Goltho
Great Gonerby
Great Tows
Grebby
Greetwell
Grimoldby
Hameringham
Hannah
Harlaxton
Hatcliffe
Healing
Heckington
Helpringham

Heydour
  Hogsthorpe
Hop Pole
  Horbling
Hough on the Hill
  Ingoldmels
Jerusalem
  Kettlethorpe
Killingholme
  Kirkby cum Osgodby
Kirmond le Mire
  Laceby
Langrick
  Laughterton
Laughton
  Leake Common Side
Legbourne
  Loosegate
Limber Magna
  Little Steeping
Martin Dales
  Mavis Enderby
Melton Ross
  Messingham
Minting
  Muckton
Mumby
  Nettleham
Nettleton
  New York

No Mans Friend
  North Cockerington
North Elkington
  Norton Disney
Old Bolingbroke
  Old Clee
Old Leake
  Owmby by Spital
Oxcombe
  Panton
Penny Hill
  Pinchbeck
Pode Hole
  Postland
Potter Hanworth
  Quadring
Ranby
  Rand-cum-Fulnery
Rippingdale
  Roughton
Roxby with Risby
  Ruckland
Saltfleetby
  Saracen's Head
Sausthorpe
  Scamblesby
Scartho
  Scopwick
Scott Willoughby
  Scotton

Scrane End
  Scremby
Scrivelsby
  Silk Willoughby
Sixhills
  Skegness
Skidbrooke with Saltfleet
  Haven
Skinnand
  Snelland
Snitterby
  Somersby
Sotby
  Sots Hole
South Somercoates
  Spital in the Street
Stain
  Stainton le Vale
Stenigot
  Stewton
Stixwould
  Stragglethorpe
Strubby
  Swallow
Swineshead
  Swinhope
Tattershall
  Temple Bruer
Theddlethorpe
  Thimbleby

Thoresway
  Thornton Curtis
Threekingham
  Throckenholt
Timberland
  Tongue End
Torksey
  Twenty
Tydd Gote
  Uffington
Usselby
  Utterby
Wainfleet
  Walesby
Wasps Nest
  Well
Whaplode Drove
  Wigtoft
Wildmore Fen
  Winceby
Winteringham
  Wispington
Withcall
  Wragby
Wrangle
  Wroot

7 things to know about Lincolnshire dialect

1. It's packed with agricultural history

Lincolnshire's rich agricultural heritage is reflected in its dialect. As you may have noticed from the glossary at the beginning of this book, many of the words sadly became redundant when agricultural machinery replaced the old way of doing things.

2. The local council wants to save it

As with dialect in other parts of the country, 'Linkisheer dialect' is in danger of being forgotten by many local people. Fortunately, it has a number of local champions, determined to keep the local lingo alive. One of these, Loretta Rivett, provides workshops to help local people understand their dialect. The local council was so concerned about local residents not understanding their own dialect that they arranged the free workshops!

3. It's got the support of Farmer Wink

Lincolnshire dialect has its very own farmer-advocate. Read more about Farmer Wink later on in this book!

4. It's in the dictionary

While Lincolnshire dialect is still at risk, some words have been captured in the Oxford English Dictionary. These include *durn* (door-post), *glore* (gaze intently), *gawn* (stare vacantly), *kelter* (rubbish), *mumping* (begging) and *paigle* (cowslip).

5. It has a dedicated dialect society

The local lingo is so important to residents that East Lincolnshire has its own dialect society. **Far Welter'd** (aka *The East Lincs Dialect Society*) aims to raise people's awareness of Lincolnshire dialect and highlight the part that it has played in their local heritage. The society makes recordings of dialect speakers to build up a multimedia archive of Lincolnshire dialect. It also brings local people together to perform the dialect material in the form of poetry readings, songs, anecdotes and audio and video recordings.

6. Some words have been rediscovered

The recent discovery of an old book has led to the recovery of some great old Lincolnshire words and sayings. In 2009, *The Wonder of Whiffling* by London author, ADAM JACOT DE BOINOD, was published. He looked at documents from Victorian county lexicographers and uncovered the local words. The national press covered the exciting new discoveries of interesting slang and regional English words, old and new.

7. Look out for local differences

As you would expect, there are variations of the Lincolnshire dialect, depending on which part of the county you're in. One version which is particularly well recognised is the Scunthorpe dialect. Locals use words such as *'bread cake'* when they're referring to a bun, *'circle'* when they're talking about a roundabout and *'tenfoot'* for an alleyway.

Barton Ladies' Hockey Team, pictured in around 1900
©North Lincolnshire Museums Service

Who is Farmer Wink?

'Farmer Wink is a Yellerbelly Phenomenon – and as any body from between the Wash and the Humber knows, that means he comes from Lincolnshire. Wink is a man of the land whose comments in the local dialect on farming, the countryside, food and, well, just

about everything, brought him to fame after he started 'phoning the local radio station with his views. His remarks and his language struck a chord with the listeners, and made him very popular, and much in demand at local charity events.'

Excerpt from introduction on Farmer Wink's YouTube channel

Farmer Wink is known as Lincolnshire's foremost 'dialect champion'! This farmer from Minting is a character created by ROBERT CARLTON and is well known for his use of traditional Lincolnshire dialect. In fact, Farmer Wink is as proud of his local dialect as he is of his home county. He became a celebrity after phoning in to Radio Lincolnshire's breakfast show. He then went on to gain a regular slot on the show and has also featured in a number of videos. One particularly popular video was the one which showed his first trip on a train to London, as organised by BBC Radio Lincolnshire. The video featured appearances from DAVID CAMERON and STEVE WRIGHT. Farmer Wink's voice is even available for satnavs, allowing you to reach your destination guided by the Lincolnshire dialect!

Essential to the war effort

It may seem surprising considering its rural roots, but Lincolnshire played an essential part in the history of the tank. In fact, it was the county's agricultural history that helped to shape the development of this military contribution. As far back as 1915, agricultural engineers William Foster and Son invented the first fighting tank.

A Hawker Hurricane over Cleethorpes, July 2013 iStock

Known as 'LITTLE WILLIE', the tank was developed as a direct response to the start of the First World War. But this was just the beginning of Lincolnshire's contribution to the war effort for both world wars. In the Second World War, Lincoln went on to produce vital war goods, such as tanks, aircraft and vehicles. The city was also the location for a number of other important engineering companies, including Richard Hornsby & Sons of Grantham who were the makers of what is recognised as the world's very first diesel engine! Lincolnshire was also the birthplace of the first production line of gas turbine engines for sea and land-based energy production in the fifties.

Lincolnshire food favourites

If you're fond of food and drink, you may well know some of the classics that originate in Lincolnshire! Whether it is Lincolnshire Poacher cheese, Batemans beer or Lincolnshire sausages, the county remains recognised thanks to its contribution to the dinner tables (and drinking habits!) of people around the country.

Famous yellowbellies

The power of an apple

One yellowbelly is as famous for his association with a particular fruit as he is for his invaluable contribution to science. Hailing from Woolsthorpe near Grantham, SIR ISAAC NEWTON chose to focus on his studies instead of running the family estate as was expected of him. It's a great thing for all of us that he did because he went on to conceive the law of gravity as well as inventing the first reflecting telescope, among many other achievements. Sadly, it is very likely that the story about the apple falling on Newton's head as he sat beneath a tree is untrue. It is said that Newton was actually just looking out of the window when he happened to see the fruit drop. There are still some who think that there never was an apple-related moment of inspiration at all! Another interesting fact about Newton (besides his incredible contribution to science, of course) is that his entire political contribution during his year as a member of parliament was to speak just once – to instruct someone to close a window!

Portrait of
Sir Isaac Newton
iStock

'I do not know what I may appear to the world, but to myself I seem to have been only like a boy playing on the seashore, and diverting myself in now and then finding a smoother pebble or a prettier shell than ordinary, whilst the great ocean of truth lay all undiscovered before me.'
SIR ISAAC NEWTON

A code for success

One Lincolnshire figure has entertained many readers and TV viewers with his fictional creations. A local of Stamford, COLIN DEXTER created one of the best-loved characters of all time when he dreamt up *Inspector Morse*. Dexter wrote his hugely popular Morse novels between 1975 and 1999. They went on to become a much admired TV series from 1987 to 2000. But it might surprise you to know that this yellowbelly's first writings were General Studies textbooks! It was some spare time during a family holiday that gave him the space to start writing fiction. Dexter's contribution to literature not only won him public acclaim, but critical acclaim too. He was the recipient of a number of Crime Writers' Association awards and in 2000 was appointed an Officer of the Order of the British Empire for services to literature.

'I always drink at lunchtime. It helps my imagination.'
COLIN DEXTER, *The Dead of Jericho*

A certain prime minister

When it comes to famous yellowbellies, no mention of Lincolnshire would be complete without the mention of one of the country's most famous prime ministers. Grantham in Lincolnshire is famed to this day for being the birthplace of MARGARET THATCHER. Whatever you think of her politics, this grocer's daughter went on to become the country's first female prime minister. But aside from Thatcher's often controversial political career, here's something you may not know about this Lincolnshire local: she may have helped to invent soft-serve ice cream! After graduating from the University of Oxford with a Chemistry degree, Thatcher was employed as a research chemist at Hammersmith food maker, J. Lyons and Company. It was her team's job to get more air into the ice cream! They duly developed a softer ice cream which was cheaper to produce. Here's another surprising fact about Margaret Thatcher. If you look up the meaning of the verb *'to handbag'* in the Oxford English Dictionary, you'll find it comes from Thatcher's rather tough, direct leadership style in cabinet meetings, based directly on her ever-present handbag!

'It's passionately interesting for me that the things that I learned in a small town, in a very modest home, are just the things that I believe have won the election.'

MARGARET THATCHER

A great British actor

If you listed some of the best-known films of our time, you would probably find this yellowbelly in most of them! Hailing from Holton cum Beckering, JIM BROADBENT has become one of the pillars of the great British acting world. Described on IMDb as 'One of England's most versatile character actors', Broadbent has done his local county proud with countless awards and a career both here and in Hollywood. His career spans films as varied as Mo*ulin Rouge!*, *Bridget Jones' Diary*, *The Iron Lady*, *Cloud Atlas* and the *Harry Potter* films. While Broadbent has won many different awards for his role in film and television, he rejected an OBE in 2002 because he said he didn't feel comfortable with actors receiving royal recognition.

'I like reflecting the culture I understand best; spotting the idiosyncrasies of British people and revealing them to an audience in a way that amuses is what I find fun.'

JIM BROADBENT

A national treasure in the making?

Another yellowbelly has made her county proud thanks to a career which has seen her rise from unknown to household name. Born in Epworth, SHERIDAN SMITH has gone on to have a career which has seen her shine in diverse roles on stage and screen. Smith started out with roles in *The Royle Family* and *Two Pints of Lager and a Packet of Crisps* and went on to star in *Love Soup*, *Gavin & Stacey*, *Benidorm* and *Cilla*. Her achievements have not gone unnoticed and she was recently made an OBE!

'I'm really grateful to my parents for having the confidence in me to let me go. I was terrified I might have to slink back to the village with my tail between my legs, and treated every job as though it were my last – I still do – but fortunately, I got work and things seemed to slot into place.'

SHERIDAN SMITH

The longest-serving Poet Laureate of Great Britain and Ireland

At the Alfred Lord Tennyson poetry monument
iStock

In 1809, just six miles from Horncastle in the Wolds village of Somersby, a Lincolnshire man was born who would go on to become one of the most quoted writers to this day. From his Lincolnshire roots, ALFRED, LORD TENNYSON became a central figure in the pantheon of English literature, famed as much for being the longest-serving Poet Laureate of Great Britain and Ireland (42 years!) as he was for poems such as *'The Charge of the Light Brigade'*, *'Tears, Idle Tears'* and *'Crossing the Bar'*. QUEEN VICTORIA said that she found great solace in Tennyson's poetry after the death of Prince Albert. Tennyson didn't stop writing poetry until his death in his eighties. He was buried in Poets' Corner in London's Westminster Abbey. He is commemorated locally with the Tennyson Research Centre at Lincoln Central Library and a statue at Lincoln Cathedral.

This literary yellowbelly's influence continues to live on to this day with some of his phrases now firmly part of our everyday speech. These include *'Nature, red in tooth and claw'*, *''Tis better to have loved and lost/Than never to have loved at all'*, and *'Theirs not to reason why, / Theirs but to do and die.'* Tennyson is so much part of our language that he is said to be the ninth most frequently quoted writer in The Oxford Dictionary of Quotations!

'My strength is as the strength of ten, because my heart is pure.'
ALFRED, LORD TENNYSON

The fourth funniest woman in Britain

Like one of her fellow yellowbellies listed above, this next Lincolnshire local chose to decline an OBE in 2001. JENNIFER SAUNDERS was born in Sleaford, Lincolnshire. After meeting her other comedy half, DAWN FRENCH, Saunders became a household name. Since then, she has earned a place in the nation's heart as a comedian and actor both on TV and in films. In 2003, Saunders was listed in The Observer as one of the 50 funniest acts in British comedy. In 2005, she was named the fourth funniest woman in Britain in a poll.

'I'm my own worst critic. I could tell the critics a thing or two about my shows.'
JENNIFER SAUNDERS

A founder of computer science

Silver Street in Lincoln was the birthplace of a person who is now seen as a founding figure of computer science. Anyone who uses a computer owes a debt to the brilliance of GEORGE BOOLE. He is the creator of *Boolean logic*, the foundation of today's digital computer logic. It is thanks to Boolean algebra and binary notation that modern-day computers are possible!

Back then, George Boole was the son of a shoemaker. He

trained and worked as a teacher. But it was his extra-curricular studies which gave rise to his self-education in maths and led to the completion of his first mathematical paper in 1838.

Boole published what is now regarded as his most important paper in 1854: *'An Investigation Into the Laws of Thought, on Which are Founded the Mathematical Theories of Logic and Probabilities'*. It is this upon which much of today's computer technology is based. Boole's achievements continued and he went to become a Fellow of the Royal Society in 1857. You can visit Boole's former home in Silver Street – if you need to use the services of the solicitors which are now based there!

> *'No matter how correct a mathematical theorem may appear to be, one ought never to be satisfied that there was not something imperfect about it until it also gives the impression of being beautiful.'*

GEORGE BOOLE

Lincolnshire's past and present is so packed with famous figures that there are just too many to mention in detail here! The county has produced such greats as footballers JOE BAKER, LEE CHAPMAN, GARY CROSBY and MARK WALLINGTON, tennis star DANIEL COX and Olympic swimming medallist

PAUL PALMER. There's also the voice of the much loved 1960s children's TV series *The Magic Roundabout*, ERIC THOMPSON, as well as lyricist BERNIE TAUPIN and comedian ROBERT WEBB.

Gurnell Street School in Scunthorpe, decorated for a tea to celebrate the Coronation of Edward VII on 9 August 1901
©North Lincolnshire Museums Service

Say what? Surprising facts about Lincolnshire

Documenting history

Did you know that Lincolnshire is the only place to hold copies of two important historical documents, the **Magna Carta** (1215) and the **Charter of the Forest** (1217)

Sinners of Bourne

The men of Bourne in Lincolnshire were immortalised in

a rather controversial way as far back as the 12th century in a work by a Gilbertine monk called ROBERT MANNYNG or ROBERT DE BRUNNE. He was a writer who spent most of his life at Sempringham, near Bourne and his most famous work, *Handlyng Synne* (Handling Sin) was about the men of Bourne! This religious manual was adapted from WILLIAM OF WADINGTON'S *Manuel des péchés* and illustrated the vices of man. Robert Mannyng is recognised to this day for helping to put the speech of everyday people into a more accessible form.

Brilliant for bulbs

Any keen gardeners out there are likely to have benefited from Lincolnshire's long heritage as the home of the bulb. More accurately, Spalding, or *'The Heart of the Fens'* as it is fondly known, continues its long tradition as the core of the bulb industry right up to this day. If you've planted bulbs in your garden, it's very likely that they'll have come from Lincolnshire!

England's first female bobby

Grantham isn't only famous for giving us the country's first female prime minister. It is also recognised for giving us the first female police officer. MRS EDITH SMITH from Grantham was appointed as the first woman police constable with full power of arrest in England in November 1914. It was her job to respond to cases in which women were involved.

A sweeping achievement

Lincolnshire is the home of the Royal Air Force Aerobatic Team, which you probably know better as the **Red Arrows**. The Red Arrows are the public face of the Royal Air Force and are rightly acknowledged as one of the world's premier aerobatic teams. They have been based at RAF Scampton in Lincolnshire since 2001.

iStock

The first North Sea energy find

Here's another Lincolnshire first for you: Britain's first North Sea energy find was made off Grimsby in 1965! It was the drilling rig Sea Gem (converted from a barge) that discovered natural gas under the sea bed 40 miles east of the Lincolnshire port. Sadly, this story also involves a tragic first: the rig was involved in the first North Sea rig disaster. Two of its legs collapsed and 13 men were killed in December in the same year.

Forbidden fruit?

It is to Stamford in Lincolnshire that we owe a first in the world of fruit and veg. The conservatory of the 16th-century Burghley House near Stamford was where the very first tomatoes were grown in the UK. Ironically, it is highly unlikely that those first tomatoes would have been enjoyed as they were believed to be poisonous in this country until about the 18th century.

Training for the Dambusters

You've probably heard of the Dambusters, but did you know that it was the Petwood Hotel at Woodhall Spa which was the Officers' Mess for 617 Squadron? The hotel was originally requisitioned by the RAF in 1942 and went on to be used by two other squadrons. However, the building (along with Woodhall Airfield) was seen as being suitably remote for the squadron's training for their important and secret work.

A seriously festive city

Did you know that Lincoln is known for being seriously festive because it hosts one of the largest Christmas markets in Europe? In fact, it is known to be a draw to no fewer than 250,000 over the four days of its run. Since the fair started in 1982, the volume of visitors has reached such a height that during the market weekend, the city sets up a circular one-way system for pedestrians and charter trains are organised from around Britain!

A horsey history

Brigg in Lincolnshire is home to the second largest horse fair in the UK. **Brigg Horse Fair** dates back all the way to 1235. On the first Saturday in August every year, Brigg is the focus of attention for buyers and sellers of horses. Organised by members of the travelling community, it's also an important meeting point for Roma and Irish travellers. The fair has been immortalised in the well-known folk song, 'Brigg Fair'.

It was on the fifth of August-er' the weather fine and fair,
Unto Brigg Fair I did repair, for love I was inclined.
I rose up with the lark in the morning, with my heart so full of glee,
Of thinking there to meet my dear, long time I'd wished to see.
Excerpt from *Brigg Fair*

A vital RAF base

Coningsby is seen by the RAF as one of their most important stations. Not only is the base home to many squadrons, it is also home to The Battle of Britain Memorial Flight (BBMF). Formed in 1957 as a tribute to the aviators of World War II, it regularly flies Spitfires and Hurricanes.

The birthplace of the Methodist movement

It is to the Lincolnshire town of Epworth that we owe the start of the Methodist movement. Epworth is the birthplace of the Wesley family who went on to found the movement.

A sweet heritage

Love chocolate? Then you might like to know that Gainsborough was the home of the **Rose brothers**. The brothers invented the first packaging machines. Their name is immortalised to this day in the name for 'Roses' chocolates.

An impish heritage

You wouldn't normally expect a mythical creature to connect a city, a cathedral and a football club, yet this is the case for the **Lincoln imp!** The figure of the imp can be found in Lincoln Cathedral on the south side of the most north-easterly pillar of its Angel Choir. An old legend dating back to the 14th century tells the tale of two imps sent by Satan to cause mayhem on Earth. They ended up doing just that at Lincoln Cathedral and one was turned to stone by a protective angel while the other escaped. In the 19th century, a Lincoln jeweller presented the Prince of Wales with an imp cravat pin. Soon after, the Prince won at the races and made a joke about the imp being behind his success. It was then that the imp's identity as the mascot of Lincoln became firmly established. Nowadays, the imp is the symbol of Lincoln while the Lincoln City Football Club are known as the Red Imps!

The finest in England?

Where's a special place to live? It could well be **Stamford**, which is regularly named as a finalist in The Sunday Times *'Britain's best place to live'* survey. Stamford was also described as *'The finest stone town in England'* by SIR WALTER SCOTT.

Sources

http://inbarton.atwebpages.com/dialect.htm

https://archive.org/stream/aglossarywordsu00colegoog/
aglossarywordsu00colegoog_djvu.txt

http://www.scribd.com/doc/92270787/Farmer-Wink#scribd

http://www.lincstothepast.com/exhibitions/historic-
environment-record/buildings/

http://churchfarmvillage.org.uk/withern-cottage/

http://www.warwickmopfair.co.uk/

http://www.theodora.com/encyclopedia/h2/hiring.html

http://www.lookandlearn.com/blog/25200/there-have-
been-fairs-in-britain-since-mediaeval-times/

http://www.fwi.co.uk/farm-life/audio-project-captures-
lincolnshires-heritage-in-rural-voices+.htm

http://www.telegraph.co.uk/news/newstopics/
howaboutthat/10211951/Council-offers-dialect-workshops-
to-residents-baffled-by-local-language.html

http://www.lincolnshire.gov.uk/OrganisationDetails.
aspx?orgcode=5183

http://www.lincolnshireecho.co.uk/Dialect-book-unearths-
lost-Lincolnshire-words/story-11222160-detail/story.html

Available now

Black Country Dialect

Bristol Dialect

Cockney Dialect

Cornish Dialect

Derbyshire Dialect

Devon Dialect

Dorset Dialect

Essex Dialect

Evolving English WordBank

Glaswegian Dialect

Hampshire Dialect

Kentish Dialect

Lancashire Dialect

Liverpool Dialect

Manchester Dialect

Newcastle upon Tyne
Dialect

Norfolk Dialect

Nottinghamshire Dialect

Scottish Dialects

Somerset Dialect

Suffolk Dialect

Sussex Dialect

Warwickshire Dialect

Wiltshire Dialect

Yorkshire Dialect

Coming in 2015

Co Durham Dialect

Gloucestershire Dialect

The Lake District Dialect

Leicestershire Dialect

Welsh Borders Dialect

**See website for
more details:
bradwellbooks.com**